The Rock Woman
SELECTED POEMS

James K. Baxter

The Rock Woman
SELECTED POEMS

LONDON
OXFORD UNIVERSITY PRESS
New York Wellington

Oxford University Press, Ely House, London W.1

GLASGOW NEW YORK TORONTO MELBOURNE WELLINGTON
CAPE TOWN SALISBURY IBADAN NAIROBI LUSAKA ADDIS ABABA
BOMBAY CALCUTTA MADRAS KARACHI LAHORE DACCA
KUALA LUMPUR SINGAPORE HONG KONG TOKYO

First published 1969
Reprinted 1971

SET IN GREAT BRITAIN AND
REPRODUCED LITHOGRAPHICALLY IN
NEW ZEALAND BY WRIGHT & CARMAN, TRENTHAM

PREFACE

This selection contains several poems unpublished
before in any book of mine, and a number which had
only been published in periodicals; but its main purpose
is to provide a reasonable sampling of my verse of the
past twenty years. Such a selection can be regarded
perhaps as a milestone. I trust it is not also a tomb-
stone. Though acknowledgements are due to many
editors and periodicals, these have already been re-
corded in the books from which previously published
poems have been taken, and I wish only to acknow-
ledge the publishers of my books: *Blow, Wind of
Fruitfulness* (Caxton Press, 1948), *On Falcon House*
(Caxton Press, 1953), *The Fallen House* (Caxton Press,
1953), *In Fires of No Return* (O.U.P., 1958), *Howrah
Bridge and Other Poems* (O.U.P., 1961), *Pig Island
Letters* (O.U.P., 1966).

In order to make this selection I have had to go
through twenty-seven unedifying manuscript books,
and was struck by the evidence they provided of an
obsessive industry that led me as often as not into the
cactus. If I have at times written well, it was hardly by
natural aptitude; and I must thank the man-killing
Muse for the care she has taken of her idiot son.

J.K.B.

CONTENTS

LOVE-LYRIC V

Seaweed in
salt swell glisters;
in brown content cool through water-walls;
negress-naiad.
   Sea still as a ballroom floor
whereon wind-centaurs caper.
The burnished golden hills
raise their wide motionless arms and sigh;
their sapless breasts caressed by haze.
   Smoke shimmers from
   chimney-pots.
Bathers like posts of
derelict wharves
on beaches forget their deaths.
. The geometric pattern is apparent.
Past modern houses
of lime and pasteboard
with windows scissored
a truck climbs, breaking the metre of the morning.
   The continual salt whisper
is no longer
treacherous; though arcs of current like sea-
serpents. . . . The twisted rock of clouds
whitens sky with dusty debris.
   Animals move
because they must
when the sun goads them from their cave of dust.
   The page is
turned, tamped down; like plague-
pits may burst from earth again
rotten and rich. But now not so.
   Flowers of foam
from undersea yeast risen.
I cannot capture

1

the mood and mould of the morning
save that it is gauche, yet
graceful: will learn life alas from violence.

LOVE-LYRIC IX

Pillars of rain on livid sea fall;
immense cloudbursts bearing
the walls of wind upon their knotted shoulders.
   The blown sea soughing
flings gulls and spume
from the muffled explosion
of toppling marble.
   Rain walks over the deep currents;
gum-leaf-coloured.
   The reefs blow through their snouts.
   Why the inane anger
   of posturing boughs?
Hawthorn berries are shaken
dumbly protesting;
and the white undersides of leaves
stream ghostlike.
   Why the inane anger?
   the whorl and ruck of cloud-rack.
   There is no anger.
Only the pulsation of electronic vigour;
the hurricane incidental as a spider-net.
The world seen in glass of time
posturing in apparent love
posturing in apparent hate
distortions only
moon-mountains under eyelids.
   Hate and love behind the eyes are real.

SEA NOON

The grey smoke of rain drifts over headlands
And clear drops fall on the paper as I write.
Only the light thunder and murmur
Of ebbing and flowing furrows is endlessly repeated
And the rapid gulls flash over without sound.

Where is a house with windows open to the afternoon?
With light beer on tables and tobacco smoke
Floating; with a fire in the grate;
With music and the mind-filling pleasure of easy
    company.
Lying back in a chair to laugh or standing and smiling
One would accept all fates, and even the gold
Melancholy leaves of late autumn
Would seem as natural as a child's toy.

But labour and hunger strides the year
In seasonal repetition, more harsh than tidal waters.
The very rocks are cold: and they were lava once.

So stand the dull green trees bearing the weather
On solitary boughs; so the grey smoke of rain
Drifts on a painted verge of sea and air.
The fisherman casts his net to hold the tide.
Chilly the light wind blowing. And dark the face of
    noonday
As at the inconsolable parting of friends.

THE BAY

On the road to the bay was a lake of rushes
Where we bathed at times and changed in the bamboos.
Now it is rather to stand and say:
How many roads we take that lead to Nowhere,
The alley overgrown, no meaning now but loss:
Not that veritable garden where everything comes easy.

And by the bay itself were cliffs with carved names
And a hut on the shore beside the maori ovens.
We raced boats from the banks of the pumice creek
Or swam in those autumnal shallows
Growing cold in amber water, riding the logs
Upstream, and waiting for the *taniwha*.

So now I remember the bay and the little spiders
On driftwood, so poisonous and quick.
The carved cliffs and the great outcrying surf
With currents round the rocks and the birds rising.
A thousand times an hour is torn across
And burned for the sake of going on living.
But I remember the bay that never was
And stand like stone and cannot turn away.

THE CAVE

In a hollow of the fields, where one would least ex-
    pect it,
Stark and suddenly this limestone buttress:
A tree whose roots are bound about the stones,
Broad-leaved, hides well that crevice at the base
That leads, one guesses, to the sunless kingdom
Where souls endure the ache of Proserpine.

Entering where no man it seemed
Had come before, I found a rivulet
Beyond the rock door running in the dark.
Where it sprang from in the heart of the hill
No one could tell: alone
It ran like Time there in the dank silence.

I spoke once and my voice resounded
Among the many pillars. Further in
Were bones of sheep that strayed and died
In nether darkness, brown and water-worn.
The smell of earth was like a secret language
That dead men speak and we have long forgotten.

The whole weight of the hill hung over me.
Gladly I would have stayed there and been hidden
From every beast that moves beneath the sun,
From age's enmity and love's contagion:
But turned and climbed back to the barrier,
Pressed through and came to dazzling daylight out.

LET TIME BE STILL

Let Time be still
Who takes all things,
Face, feature, memory
Under his blinding wings.

That I hold again the green
Larch of your body
Whose leaves will gather
The springs of the sky.

And fallen from his cloud
The falcon find
The thigh-encompassed wound
Breasts silken under hand.

Though in a dark room
We knew the day breaking
And the rain-bearing wind
Cold matins making.

Sure it seemed
That hidden away
From the sorrowful wind
In deep bracken I lay.

Your mouth was the sun
And green earth under
The rose of your body flowering
Asking and tender
In the timelost season
Of perpetual summer.

HAAST PASS

In the dense bush all leaves and bark exude
The odour of mortality; for plants
Accept their death like stones
Rooted for ever in time's torrent bed.

Return from here. We have nothing to learn
From the dank falling of fern spores
Or the pure glacier blaze that melts
Down mountains, flowing to the Tasman.

This earth was never ours. Remember
Rather the tired faces in the pub
The children who have never grown. Return
To the near death, the loves like garden flowers.

ELEGY FOR
MY FATHER'S FATHER

He knew in the hour he died
That his heart had never spoken
In eighty years of days.
O for the tall tower broken
Memorial is denied:
And the unchanging cairn
That pipes could set ablaze
An aaronsrod and blossom.
They stood by the graveside
From his bitter veins born
And mourned him in their fashion.
A chain of sods in a day
He could slice and build
High as the head of a man
And a flowering cherry tree
On his walking shoulder held
Under the lion sun.
When he was old and blind
He sat in a curved chair
All day by the kitchen fire.
Many hours he had seen
The stars in their drunken dancing
Through the burning-glass of his mind
And sober knew the green
Boughs of heaven folding
The winter world in their hand.
The pride of his heart was dumb.
He knew in the hour he died
That his heart had never spoken
In song or bridal bed.
And the naked thought fell back
To a house by the waterside
And the leaves the wind had shaken
Then for a child's sake:

To the waves all night awake
With the dark mouths of the dead.
The tongues of water spoke
And his heart was unafraid.

ELEGY FOR AN UNKNOWN SOLDIER

There was a time when I would magnify
His ending; scatter words as if I wept
Tears not my own but man's. There was a time.
But not now so. He died of a common sickness.

Nor did any new star shine
Upon that day when he came crying out
Of fleshy darkness to a world of pain
And waxen eyelids let the daylight enter.

So felt and tasted, found earth good enough.
Later he played with stones and wondered
If there was land beyond the dark sea rim
And where the road led out of the farthest paddock.

Awkward at school, he could not master sums.
Could you expect him then to understand
The miracle and menace of his body
That grew as mushrooms grow from dusk to dawn?

He had the weight though for a football scrum
And thought it fine to listen to the cheering
And drink beer with the boys, telling them tall
Stories of girls that he had never known.

So when the War came he was glad and sorry,
But soon enlisted. Then his mother cried
A little, and his father boasted how
He'd let him go, though needed for the farm.

Likely in Egypt he would find out something
About himself, if flies and drunkenness
And deadly heat could tell him much—until
In his first battle a shell splinter caught him.

So crown him with memorial bronze among
The older dead, child of a mountainous island.
Wings of a tarnished victory shadow him
Who born of silence has burned back to silence.

VIRGINIA LAKE

The lake lies blind and glinting in the sun.
Among the reeds the red-billed native birds
Step high like dancers. I have found
A tongue to praise them, who was dumb,
And from the deaf morass one word
Breaks with the voices of the numberless drowned.

This was the garden and the talking water
Where once a child walked and wondered
At the leaves' treasure house, the brown ducks riding
Over the water face, the four winds calling
His name aloud, and a green world under
Where fish like stars in a fallen heaven glided.

And for his love the eyeless statues moved
Down the shell paths. The bandstand set
On fire with music blazing at its centre
Was havened in his love.
The lichened elm was rafters overhead,
Old waves unlocked their gates for him to enter.

Who now lies dumb, the black tongue dry
And the eyes weighed with coins.
O out of this rock tomb
Of labyrinthine grief I start and cry
Toward his real day—the undestroyed
Fantastic Eden of a waking dream.

ROCKET SHOW

As warm north rain breaks over suburb houses,
Streaming on window glass, its drifting hazes
Covering harbour ranges with a dense hood:
I recall how eighteen months ago I stood
Ankle-deep in sand on an Otago beach
Watching the fireworks flare over strident surf and
    bach,
In brain grey ash, in heart the sea-change flowing
Of one love dying and another growing.

For love grows like the crocus bulb in winter
Hiding from snow and from itself the tender
Green frond in embryo; but dies as rockets die
(White sparks of pain against a steel-dark sky)
With firebird wings trailing an arc of grief
Across a night inhuman as the grave,
Falling at length a dull and smouldering shell
To frozen dunes and the wash of the quenching
    swell.

There was little room left where the crowd had
    trampled
Grass and lupin bare, under the pines that trembled
In gusts from the sea. On a sandhillock I chose
A place to watch from. Then the rockets rose,
O marvellous, like self-destroying flowers
On slender stems, with seed-pods full of flares,
Raining down amber, scarlet, pennies from heaven
On the skyward straining heads and still sea-haven.
Had they brought death, we would have stood the
    same,
I think, in ecstasy at the world-end flame.

It is the rain streaming reminds me of
Those ardent showers, cathartic love and grief.
As I walked home through the cold streets by moon-
    light,
My steps ringing in the October night,
I thought of our strange lives, the grinding cycle
Of death and renewal come to full circle,
And of man's heart, that blind Rosetta stone,
Mad as the polar moon, decipherable by none.

WILD BEES

Often in summer, on a tarred bridge plank standing,
Or downstream between willows, a safe Ophelia
    drifting
In a rented boat—I had seen them come and go,
Those wild bees swift as tigers, their gauze wings
    a-glitter
In passionless industry, clustering black at the crevice
Of a rotten cabbage tree, where their hive was hidden
    low.

But never strolled too near. Till one half-cloudy
    evening
Of ripe January, my friends and I
Came, gloved and masked to the eyes like plundering
    desperadoes,
To smoke them out. Quiet beside the stagnant river
We trod wet grasses down, hearing the crickets chitter
And waiting for light to drain from the wounded sky.

Before we reached the hive their sentries saw us
And sprang invisible through the darkening air,
Stabbed, and died in stinging. The hive woke. Poison-
    ous fuming
Of sulphur filled the hollow trunk, and crawling
Blue flame sputtered—yet still their suicidal
Live raiders dived and clung to our hands and hair.

O it was Carthage under the Roman torches,
Or loud with flames and falling timber, Troy!
A job well botched. Half of the honey melted
And half the rest young grubs. Through earth-black
    smouldering ashes
And maimed bees groaning, we drew out our plunder.
Little enough their gold, and slight our joy.

16

Fallen then the city of instinctive wisdom.
Tragedy is written distinct and small:
A hive burned on a cool night in summer.

But loss is a precious stone to me, a nectar
Distilled in time, preaching the truth of winter
To the fallen heart that does not cease to fall.

POEM IN THE MATUKITUKI VALLEY

Some few yards from the hut the standing beeches
Let fall their dead limbs, overgrown
With feathered moss and filigree of bracken.
The rotted wood splits clean and hard
Close-grained to the driven axe, with sound of water
Sibilant falling and high nested birds.

In winter blind with snow; but in full summer
The forest blanket sheds its cloudy pollen
And cloaks a range in undevouring fire.
Remote the land's heart. Though the wild scrub cattle
Acclimatised, may learn
Shreds of her purpose, or the taloned kea.

For those who come as I do, half-aware,
Wading the swollen
Matukituki waist-high in snow water,
And stumbling where the mountains throw their dice
Of boulders huge as houses, or the smoking
Cataract flings its arrows on our path—

For us the land is matrix and destroyer,
Resentful, darkly known
By sunset omens, low words heard in branches;
Or where the red deer lift their innocent heads
Snuffing the wind for danger,
And from our footfall's menace bound in terror.

Three emblems of the heart I carry folded
As charms against flood water, sliding shale:
Pale gentian, lily, and bush orchid.
The peaks too have names to suit their whiteness,
Stargazer and Moonraker,
A sailor's language and a mountaineer's.

And those who sleep in close bags fitfully
Besieged by wind in a snowline bivouac—
The carrion parrot with red underwing
Clangs on the roof by night, and daybreak brings
Raincloud on purple ranges, light reflected
Stainless from crumbling glacier, dazzling snow.

Do they not, clay in that unearthly furnace,
Endure the hermit's peace
And mindless ecstasy? Blue-lipped crevasse
And smooth rock chimney straddling—a communion
With what eludes our net, Leviathan
Stirring to ocean birth our inland waters?

Sky's purity; the altar cloth of snow
On deathly summits laid; or avalanche
That shakes the rough moraine with giant laughter;
Snowplume and whirlwind—what are these
But His flawed mirror who gave the mountain strength
And dwells in holy calm, undying freshness?

Therefore we turn, hiding our souls' dullness
From that too blinding glass: turn to the gentle
Dark of the human daydream, child and wife,
Patience of stone and soil, the lawful city
Where man may live, and no wild trespass
Of what's eternal shake his grave of time.

THE HOMECOMING

Odysseus has come home, to the gully farm
Where the macrocarpa windbreak shields a house
Heavy with time's reliques—the brown-filmed photo-
    graphs
Of ghosts more real than he; the mankind-measuring
    arm
Of a pendulum clock; and true yet to her vows,
His mother, grief's Penelope. At the blind the sea wind
    laughs.

The siege more long and terrible than Troy's
Begins again. A love demanding all,
Hypochondriacal, sea-dark and contentless:
This was the sour ground that nurtured a boy's
Dream of freedom; this, in Circe's hall
Drugged him; his homecoming finds this, more
    relentless.

She does not say, 'You have changed'; nor could she
    imagine any
Otherwise to the quiet maelstrom spinning
In the circle of their days. Still she would wish to carry
Him folded within her, shut from the wild and many
Voices of life's combat, in the cage of beginning;
She counts it natural that he should never marry.

She will cook his meals; complain of the south weather
That wrings her joints. And he—rebels; and yields
To the old covenant—calms the bleating
Ewe in birth travail. The smell of saddle leather
His sacrament; or the sale day drink; yet hears beyond
    sparse fields
On reef and cave the sea's hexameter beating.

ELEGY AT THE YEAR'S END

At the year's end I come to my father's house
Where passion fruit hang gold above an open doorway
And garden trees bend to the visiting bird:
    Here first the single vision
Entered my heart, as to a dusty room
Enters the pure tyrannical wind of heaven.

The coal burns out; the quiet ash remains
That tired minds and coarsened bodies know.
    Small town of corrugated iron roofs
Between the low volcanic saddle
And offshore reef where blue cod browse,
From husks of exile, humbled, I come to your fond
    prison.

At an elder uncle's deathbed I read the graph
Of suffering in the face of country cousins.
    These have endured what men hold in common,
The cross of custom, the marriage bed of knives;
Their angular faces reflecting his
Whose body lies stiff under the coverlet.

One may walk again to the fisherman's rock, hearing
The long waves tumble, from America riding
Where mottled kelpbeds heave to a pale sun,
    But not again see green Aphrodite
Rise to transfigure the noon. Rather the Sophoclean
Chorus: *All shall be taken.*

Or by the brown lagoon stand idle
Where to their haunted coves the safe flocks go,
And envy the paradise drake his brilliant sexual plum-
    age.
    For single vision dies. Spirit and flesh are sundered
In the kingdom of no love. Our stunted passions bend
To serve again familiar social devils.

Brief is the visiting angel. In corridors of hunger
Our lives entwined suffer the common ill:
Living and dying, breathing and begetting.
Meanwhile on maimed gravestones under the towering
    fennel
Moves the bright lizard, sunloved, basking in
    The moment of animal joy.

LAMENT FOR BARNEY FLANAGAN
Licensee of the Hesperus Hotel

Flanagan got up on a Saturday morning,
Pulled on his pants while the coffee was warming;
He didn't remember the doctor's warning,
   'Your heart's too big, Mr. Flanagan.'

Barney Flanagan, sprung like a frog
From a wet root in an Irish bog—
May his soul escape from the tooth of the dog!
   God have mercy on Flanagan.

Barney Flanagan R.I.P.
Rode to his grave on Hennessey's
Like a bottle-cork boat in the Irish Sea.
   The bell-boy rings for Flanagan.

Barney Flanagan, ripe for a coffin,
Eighteen stone and brandy-rotten,
Patted the housemaid's velvet bottom—
   'Oh, is it you, Mr. Flanagan?'

The sky was bright as a new milk token.
Bill the Bookie and Shellshock Hogan
Waited outside for the pub to open—
   'Good day, Mr. Flanagan.'

At noon he was drinking in the lounge bar corner
With a sergeant of police and a racehorse owner
When the Angel of Death looked over his shoulder—
   'Could you spare a moment, Flanagan?'

Oh the deck was cut; the bets were laid;
But the very last card that Barney played
Was the Deadman's Trump, the bullet of Spades—
   'Would you like more air, Mr. Flanagan?'

The priest came running but the priest came late
For Barney was banging at the Pearly Gate.
St. Peter said, 'Quiet! You'll have to wait
    For a hundred masses, Flanagan.'

The regular boys and the loud accountants
Left their nips and their seven-ounces
As chickens fly when the buzzard pounces—
    'Have you heard about old Flanagan?'

Cold in the parlour Flanagan lay
Like a bride at the end of her marriage day.
The Waterside Workers' Band will play
    A brass goodbye to Flanagan.

While publicans drink their profits still,
While lawyers flock to be in at the kill,
While Aussie barmen milk the till
    We will remember Flanagan.

For Barney had a send-off and no mistake.
He died like a man for his country's sake;
And the Governor-General came to his wake.
    Drink again to Flanagan!

Despise not, O Lord, the work of Thine own hands
And let light perpetual shine upon him.

CROSSING COOK STRAIT

The night was clear, sea calm; I came on deck
To stretch my legs, find perhaps
Gossip, a girl in green slacks at the rail
Or just the logline feathering a dumb wake.

The ship swung in the elbow of the Strait.
'Dolphins!' I cried—'let the true sad Venus
Rise riding her shoals, teach me as once to wonder
And wander at ease, be glad and never regret.'

But night increased under the signal stars.
In the dark bows, facing the flat sea,
Stood one I had not expected, yet knew without sur-
    prise
As the Janus made formidable by loveless years.

His coat military; his gesture mild—
'Well met,' he said, 'on the terrestrial journey
From chaos into light—what light it is
Contains our peril and purpose, history has not re-
    vealed.'

'Sir—', I began. He spoke with words of steel—
'I am Seddon and Savage, the socialist father.
You have known me only in my mask of Dionysus
Amputated in bar rooms, dismembered among wheels.

'I woke in my civil tomb hearing a shout
For bread and justice. It was not here.
That sound came thinly over the waves from China;
Stones piled on my grave had all but shut it out.

'I walked forth gladly to find the angry poor
Who are my nation; discovered instead
The glutton seagulls squabbling over crusts
And policies made and broken behind locked doors.

'I have watched the poets also at their trade.
I have seen them burning with a wormwood brilliance.
Love was the one thing lacking on their page,
The crushed herb of grief at another's pain.

'Your civil calm breeds inward poverty
That chafes for change. The ghost of Adam
Gibbering demoniac in drawing-rooms
Will drink down hemlock with his sugared tea.

'You feed your paupers concrete. They work well,
Ask for no second meal, vote, pay tribute
Of silence on Anzac Day in the pub urinal;
Expose death only by a mushroom smell.

'My counsel was naive. Anger is bread
To the poor, their guns more accurate than justice,
Because their love has not decayed to a wintry fungus
And hope to the wish for power among the dead.

'In Kaitangata the miner's falling sweat
Wakes in the coal seam fossil flowers.
The clerk puts down his pen and takes his coat;
He will not be back today or the next day either.'

With an ambiguous salute he left me.
The ship moved into a stronger sea,
Bludgeoned alive by the rough mystery
Of love in the running straits of history.

THE ROCK WOMAN

Here the south sea washes
Kelpbed and margin of the drumhard sand.
Its grey surf-pillars thundering
Concede no altar, no denial
But an obscure torment
At the mind's edge trembling, about to be.

Continually, as a boy, I came to this
Rock ledge above the sinuous wave
Where dogs and gulls left excrement,
As if the sea-split ground could set at ease
The wish to be no longer man
That wrenched me then, that overstrides me now.

A rock carved like a woman,
Pain's torso, guardian of the place,
Told raining beads. I did not know
What grief her look wrung dry,
In what blind rooms and tombs
I and my fellows would walk heavily.

Magdalen of the rock
Unvirgin pray for us.
In the wave's throb our agonies awake
Rise to your true all-suffering kiss.
In hewn rock of prayer
You ask for us the death hour's peace.

HOST AND STRANGER

Stranger behind the mirror
Of my fire-sundered days
True to the last cinder
Locked in the coffin bone,
In the wrong night lying
I hear your ice harp summon
From the drumming grave
No song of the summer dying
Blood-branded field of Adam,
Only the judgement stone
Of unattempted love.

Stranger with sword and mirror
Among my tangled days,
With your two-handed terror
Strike the dead folly down.
No dream of good age
Sighs from the judgement stone.
Tell me what must be known,
Shatter the serpent dream,
While in her eyeproof room
The dark inventions move
Of daylabouring love.

AT HOKIANGA

Green floating mangrove pods reveal,
Plucked from the lagging tide, their small
Man-in-a-boat, kernel and clitoris:
Set free to sail, they climb a hundred beaches,
Germinate in night-black mud. Tell,
Historian, how the broken tribes were healed
In a land of exhausted wells, north
From that great ragged capital
Flung like a coat to rot on garden earth.

In houses thatched with nikau palm,
Fearing the dead, riding bareback
On hill stallions, those who learned before us
The secret of survival, to be patient,
Suffer, and shut no doors,
Change all things to their habit, bridge
The bogs with branch laid to branch:
Nourished at compliant breasts, wish only,
To drink with friends, own a launch.

To scrape the bones of the dead, how needful,
Lest they should walk, undo forgetfulness
With blight on crops, sickness at home.
In packed ground the missionary fathers
Drowned at river crossings, rest in one bed,
While a boy cuts from flax a spirit boat
Perfect, lightly as a bird's wing
Riding the void of waters
Untaught, a full hour floating.

TO A TRAVELLING FRIEND

Friend, other self, hanging your coat
On a cabin door at one o'clock
In the thudding boat: think how Circe
Tempts, with song, then with eyes of rock.
We die with the birth-cord round the throat.
The sense of travelling on into the dark
Possesses you, as whisky mounts the senses,
As a king mounts the execution block.

Radishes (with salt) expressed her wish
For love, beyond her husband's means;
Peeled, in a covered dish.
Later on, as if seen through a lens,
The wide crabflats of afternoon
Stroked by the tide, hot and gross:
Leaving the coverlet creased on the great bed,
You dressed, thinking—'Sex destroys itself,
A scar whitened where the wound was.'

At Devonport, your hand pouring
Beer from a glass jug, under the canvas awning,
Chair tilting back, shell of oysters,
Belly laughter while the planets rage . . .

Can we grip hope, with amputated thumbs?

Where do the rough boys end? In furnished rooms
Many drink hemlock. Some, some
Lie like straws in ice, lulled
By the spider-headed queen.
Keep safe the small gold cross I gave you,
These ambiguities of friendship culled
At morning when the leaves are green.

Light ebbs on tilting jetties, night
Pressing her fingers on reddened eyes.

A PROSPECT OF OLD AGE

Suppose a nest of bees, their honey staining
Brown brittle paper on the wall:
A sun dried hut of bricks, bone-dry
Kiln for the hermit years remaining.

Let this man work entirely to recapture
The aerial music of his youth,
Or talk with angels as the carnal
Agony subsides. A stony rapture

This would be. Revengeful, as if joking,
Cheat Caesar by apparent death,
Deny his relatives their pound of flesh,
To criticise his smell, his cough, his smoking.

Let that sweet corrosive dream
More dangerous than Simeon Stylites'
Take shape: an old man at his prayers,
Self-gutted, tugged from the human stream,

An old grey gander with no goose
Who wakes in moonlight groaning for
The dead to answer. Hears above his head
The cranky shutter clatter loose.

ELEPHANTA

Accordion and sweet brisk drum
Waken a lounging passion

Outside the wooden teashop where a young
Black-trousered androgynous dancer

Trounces the dust, crooking a maggot's finger,
While pockmarked queers applaud and smoke.

Great hawks like monoplanes
Above the bony tamarind,

Above the quarried rock sail high, high,
And Shiva like a business uncle watches

The village girls with cans to fill
File through the temple to a covered cistern.

Consider. Seasnake, white cloud minnow,
Octopus and moray eel,

Lovely in their lit aquariums
Breathe water as we do,

Have the advantage that they cannot feel.
Yet I have seen, across an angry tide-rip,

The narrow coffin-boat, the catamaran,
Go simply as a girl, with forward-leaning

Mast and torn triangular sail,
Leaving a crowded net behind.

ON THE DEATH OF HER BODY

It is a thought breaking the granite heart
Time has given me, that my one treasure,
Your limbs, those passion-vines, that bamboo body

Should age and slacken, rot
Some day in a ghastly clay-stopped hole.
They led me to the mountains beyond pleasure

Where each is not gross body or blank soul
But a strong harp the wind of genesis
Makes music in, such resonant music

That I was Adam, loosened by your kiss
From time's hard bond, and you,
My love, in the world's first summer stood

Plucking the flowers of the abyss.

BALLAD OF CALVARY STREET

On Calvary Street are trellises
Where bright as blood the roses bloom,
And gnomes like pagan fetishes
Hang their hats on an empty tomb
Where two old souls go slowly mad,
National Mum and Labour Dad.

Each Saturday when full of smiles
The children come to pay their due,
Mum takes down the family files
And cover to cover she thumbs them through,
Poor Len before he went away
And Mabel on her wedding day.

The meal-brown scones display her knack,
Her polished oven spits with rage,
While in Grunt Grotto at the back
Dad sits and reads the Sporting Page,
Then ambles out in boots of lead
To weed around the parsnip bed.

A giant parsnip sparks his eye,
Majestic as the Tree of Life;
He washes it and rubs it dry
And takes it in to his old wife—
'Look, Laura, would that be a fit?
The bastard has a flange on it!'

When both were young she would have laughed,
A goddess in her tartan skirt,
But wisdom, age and mothercraft
Have rubbed it home that men like dirt:
Five children and a fallen womb,
A golden crown beyond the tomb.

Nearer the bone, sin is sin,
And women bear the cross of woe,
And that affair with Mrs. Flynn
(It happened thirty years ago)
Though never mentioned, means that he
Will get no sugar in his tea.

The afternoon goes by, goes by,
The angels harp above a cloud;
A son-in-law with spotted tie
And daughter Alice fat and loud
Discuss the virtues of insurance
And stuff their tripes with trained endurance.

Flood-waters hurl upon the dyke
And Dad himself can go to town,
For little Charlie on his trike
Has ploughed another iris down.
His parents rise to chain the beast,
Brush off the last crumbs of their lovefeast.

And so these two old fools are left,
A rosy pair in evening light,
To question Heaven's dubious gift,
To hag and grumble, growl and fight:
The love they kill won't let them rest,
Two birds that peck in one fouled nest.

Why hammer nails? Why give no change?
Habit, habit clogs them dumb.
The Sacred Heart above the range
Will bleed and burn till Kingdom Come,
But Yin and Yang won't ever meet
In Calvary Street, in Calvary Street.

from PIG ISLAND LETTERS

I

The gap you speak of—yes, I find it so,
The menopause of the mind. I think of it
As a little death, practising for the greater,
For the undertaker who won't have read
Your stories or my verse—
Or that a self had died
Who handled ideas like bombs,

In that bare southern town
At a party on a cold night
Men seen as ghosts, women like trees walking,
Seen from the floor, a forest of legs and bums
For the climbing boy, the book-bred one.

And this, the moment of art, can never stay.
Wives in the kitchen cease to smile as we go
Into the gap itself, the solid night
Where poor drunks fear the icy firmament:
Man is a walking grave,

That is where I start from. Though often
Where the Leith Stream wandered down
Its culvert, crinkled labia of blossom
On the trees beside the weir
Captured and held the fugitive
From time, from self, from the iron pyramid,

These were diversions. Give my love
To Vic. He is aware of
The albatross. In the Otago storms
Carrying spray to salt the landward farms
The wind is a drunkard. Whoever can listen
Long enough will write again.

37

2

From an old house shaded with macrocarpas
Rises my malady.
Love is not valued much in Pig Island
Though we admire its walking parody,

That brisk gaunt woman in the kitchen
Feeding the coal range, sullen
To all strangers, lest one should be
Her antique horn-red Satan.

Her man, much baffled, grousing in the pub,
Discusses sales
Of yearling lambs, the timber in a tree
Thrown down by autumn gales,

Her daughter, reading in her room
A catalogue of dresses,
Can drive a tractor, goes to Training College,
Will vote on the side of the Bosses,

Her son is moodier, has seen
An angel with a sword
Standing above the clump of old man manuka
Just waiting for the word

To overturn the cities and the rivers
And split the house like a rotten totara log.
Quite unconcerned he sets his traps for possums
And whistles to his dog.

The man who talks to the masters of Pig Island
About the love they dread
Plaits ropes of sand, yet I was born among them
And will lie some day with their dead.

3

That other Baxter the Sectarian
Said that the bodies of the damned will burn
Like stubble thrown into a red-hot oven
On Judgement Day. In Calvin's town
At seventeen I thought I might see
Not fire but water rise

From the shelves of surf beyond St. Clair
To clang the dry bell. Gripping
A pillow wife in bed
I did my convict drill,
And when I made a mother of the keg
The town split open like an owl's egg
Breaking the ladders down. It was
Perhaps the winter of beginning:

Frost standing up like stubble in the streets
Below the knees of Maori Hill,
Looking for the last simplicity
And nothing to explain it in the books,
In a room where the wind clattered the blind-cord
In the bed of a girl with long plaits
I found the point of entry,
The place where father Adam died.

Meanwhile a boy with dog and ferret
Climbed up the gorse track from the sea
To the turn at the top of the gully
Twelve paces past the cabbage tree,
And saw from the crest of the hill
Pillars of rain move on the dark sea,
A cloud of fire rise up above Japan,
God's body blazing on damnation's tree.

Thank you for the letter. I read your book
Five days ago: it has the slow
Imperceptible wingbeat of the hawk
Above the dry scrublands. The kill is there
In the Maori riverbed below
Where bones glitter. I could tell
Of other matters, but not now.

7

This love that heals like a crooked limb
In each of us, source of our grief,
Could tell us if we cared to listen, why
Sons by mayhem, daughters by harlotry
Pluck down the sky's rage on settled houses:
The thin girl and the cornerboy
Whose angers mask their love
Unwind, unwind the bandages
That hide in each the hope of joy.

For me it is the weirs that mention
The love that we destroy
By long evasion, politics and art,
And speech that is a kind of contraception:
A streetlight flashing down
On muscled water, bodies in the shade,
Tears on a moonwhite face, the voice
Of time from the grave of water speaking to
Those who are lucky to be sad.

9

Look at the simple caption of success,
The poet as family man,
Head between thumbs at mass, nailing a trolley,
Letting the tomcat in:
Then turn the hourglass over, find the other
Convict self, incorrigible, scarred
With what the bottle and the sex games taught,
The black triangle, the whips of sin.
The first gets all his meat from the skull-faced twin,
Sharpening a dagger out of a spoon,
Struggling to speak through the gags of a poem:
When both can make a third my work is done.

Nor will the obituary ever indicate
How much we needed friends,
Like Fitz at the National
Speaking of his hydatid cyst,
A football underneath the lung,
Or Lowry in Auckland: all who held the door
And gave us space for art,
Time for the re-shaping of the heart:
Those whom the arrow-makers honour least,
Companions to the manbeast,
One man in many, touching the flayed hide gently,
A brother to the artist and a nurse.

The trees rustle as October comes
And fantails batter on the glass,
Season when the day nurse tuts and hums
Laying out pills and orange juice
For one who walks the bridge of dread
As oedema sets in,
While through the bogs and gullies of Pig Island
Bellies are beaten like skin drums
In pup tents, under flax or lupin shade,

As if the sun were a keg. And this man
On the postman's round will meditate
The horn of Jacob withered at the root
Or quirks of weather. None
Grow old easily. The poem is
A plank laid over the lion's den.

11

Tonight I read my son a story
About the bees of Baiame, who tell the east wind
To blow down rain, so that the flowers grow
In dry Australia, and the crow wirinun
Who jailed the west wind in a hollow log:

My son who is able to build a tree house
With vine ladders, my son
In his brown knitted jersey and dungarees,
Makes clowns and animals, a world of creatures
To populate paradise,

And when he hands me easily
The key of entry, my joy must be dissembled
Under a shutter of horn, a dark lantern,
In case it should too brightly burn,

Because the journey has begun
Into the land where the sun is silent
And no one may enter the tree house
That hides the bones of a child in the forest of a man.

13

Stat crux dum volvitur orbis: I will sing
In the whale's belly.
                    'Great Mother of God
Sweeten my foul breath. I wait for a death.
Cradle me, Lady, on the day they carry
My body down the bush track to the road
To the rollers of the decorous van.
The leper's stump, the thick voice of the drunk,
Are knocking at Nazareth. I am a naked man.'

'How can I let you in?
The time for talk has gone;
A mountain is the threshold stone.'

'Mother, I come alone.
No books, no bread
Are left in my swag.'

'Why are your hands not clean?'

'There was no soap in the whole damned town.'

'God's grace has need of man's apology.'

'Your face is my theology.'

'Yes; but I gave you a jewel to bring.'

'In the thick gorse of the gully
I lost your signet ring.'

'Why should I listen then?'

'On Skull Hill there was none,
No scapular, no sign,
Only the words, *I thirst*,
When the blood of a convict burst
From the body of your son.'

'You may come in.'

Is it like that? At least I know no better;
After a night of argument
Mythical, theological, political,
Somebody has the sense to get a boat
And row out towards the crayfish rocks
Where, diving deep, the downward swimmer
Finds fresh water rising up,
A mounded water breast, a fountain,
An invisible tree whose roots cannot be found;

As that wild nymph of water rises
So does the God in man.

THE WATCH

That bad year when we were both apart
The statues in the churches were covered in purple
And north of Auckland I woke to see a sail-shaped rock
Standing up from the endless water. The boat
Lumbered. The stink of vomit and vodka stuck
To the craters in my brain. It isn't simple
To be oneself. The void inside
Grows troublesome. At midday a yellow bee
Flew over the hummocked waves as if he were search-
    ing
For clover in a paddock. At night the boat stopped
    lurching
And I came on deck for the graveyard watch.
Sea, air, night;
The numbers had been rubbed from the clock.
At the deck's edge a sailor in dungarees
Let down a hook and a line.
Inside my head I heard the voice of another man:

'In Circe's palace I fell drunk
Missing the steep ladder;
I came before you to this den.
Plant above my bones that oar
I used to tug, strong at the rower's bench.
When your throats are dry and the keg is empty
Remember me . . .'

WAIPATIKI BEACH

1

Under rough kingly walls the black-and-white
Sandpiper treads on stilts the edges

Of the lagoon, whose cry is like
A creaking door. We came across the ridges

By a bad road, banging in second gear,
Into the only world I love:

This wilderness. Through the noon light rambling clear
Foals and heifers in the green paddocks move.

The sun is a shepherd. Once I would have wanted
The touch of flesh to cap and seal my joy,

Not yet having sorted it out. Bare earth, bare sea,
Without fingers crack open the hard ribs of the dead.

2

If anyone, I'd say the oldest Venus
Too early for the books, ubiquitous,

The manifold mother to whom my poems go
Like ladders down—at the mouth of the gully

She had left a lip of sand for the coarse grass to grow,
Also the very quiet native bee

Loading his pollen bags. We parked the car
There, and walked on

Down to the bank of the creek, where the water ran
    under
A froth of floating sticks and pumice stone,

And saw in the dune's clasp the burnt black
Trunk of a totara the sea had rolled back.

3

Her lion face, the skull-brown Hekate
Ruling my blood since I was born,

I had not found it yet. I and my son
Went past the hundred-headed cabbage tree

At the end of the beach, barefooted, in danger of
Stones falling from the overhang, and came

On a bay too small to have a name
Where flax grew wild on the shoulder of the bluff

And a waterfall was weeping. A sheep leapt and stood
Bleating at us beyond a tangle of driftwood

And broken planks. Behind us floated in the broad noon
Sky that female ghost, the daylight moon.

4

A leper's anger in the moon's disk, or
The long-tongued breaker choked by sand,

Spell out my years like Pharaoh's wheat and husk—
I walk and look for shelter from the wind

Where many feet have trodden
Till silence rises and the beach is hidden.

AT ROTORUA

I see the skull moon reddened by
Scrub fires, a summer gorgon,

Shoot arrows down into the dream
Where golden girl and tousled boy

On creaking camp-beds tabernacled
Repeat, repeat the act of kind

As if to the bone flute of Tutanekai.
Their eyes control the dying summer,

But I am friendlier with those Puritans,
The dead who rot on single beds

Of concrete where the steam-vents rise,
Beyond misapprehension, drugs, and those

Demons of lucre and great boredom
The living cannot exorcize:

Close, close, it seems, to the neglected powers
Our lives have lost the use of,

A pain that is its own instruction,
The resignation of a stone or bone.

THE COLD HUB

Lying awake on a bench in the town belt,
Alone, eighteen, more or less alive,
Lying awake to the sound of clocks,
The railway station clock, the Town Hall clock,
And the Varsity clock, genteel, exact
As a Presbyterian conscience,
I heard the hedgehogs chugging round my bench,
Colder than an ice-axe, colder than a bone,
Sweating the booze out, a spiritual Houdini
Inside the padlocked box of winter, time and craving.

Sometimes I rolled my coat and put it under my head,
And when my back got frozen, I put it on again.
I thought of my father and mother snoring at home
While the fire burnt out in feathery embers.
I thought of my friends each in their own house
Lying under blankets, tidy as dogs or mice.
I thought of my Med. Student girlfriend
Dreaming of horses, cantering brown-eyed horses,
In her unreachable bed, wrapped in a yellow quilt,

And something bust inside me, like a winter clod
Cracked open by the frost. A sense of being at
The absolute unmoving hub
From which, to which, the intricate roads went.
Like Hemingway, I call it *nada*:
Nada, the Spanish word for nothing.
Nada; the belly of the whale; *nada*;
Nada; the little hub of the great wheel;
Nada; the house on Cold Mountain
Where the east and the west wall bang together;
Nada; the drink inside the empty bottle.
You can't get there unless you are there.
The hole in my pants where the money falls out,
That's the beginning of knowledge; *nada*.

It didn't last for long; it never left me.
I knew that I was *nada*. Almost happy,
Stiff as a giraffe, I called in later
At an early grill, had coffee, chatted with the boss.
That night, drunk again, I slept much better
At the bus station, in a broom cupboard.

THE HARLOT

It is the body of the young harlot
Somewhere, I forget just where I saw it—
Above a doorway of the cathedral at Chartres
Or it might have been at Rheims—
Naked and beautiful, a very human beauty
And therefore a beauty whose meaning is pity,
Carried shoulder-high
By the hawk-headed demons.

The long hair, the face tilted up to the sky
As if waiting for rain to fall,
The breasts, the bone cage of the ribs,
The soft pouch of generation,
The collarbone—yes, the collarbone in particular—
And her arms hanging slack
Like someone carried on a bier.

'I thought you might be here', she said,
And smiled the broad smile I had seen before.

A TAKAPUNA BUSINESS MAN
CONSIDERS HIS SON'S DEATH
IN KOREA

Your sailboat yawns for you in the spidery shed
Among the mangrove trunks; I watched you build it
Before they hid you under stones in a pit
In North Korean ice. Your mother's head,

High cheekbones, hard black eyes! At Cherry Farm
She waits for God, a tube-fed schizophrene
With the unwrinkled forehead of eighteen.
The harbour's death-mask sweats in summer calm.

In my wall safe I keep the fir tree cone
You gave me once. You liked your whisky-mad
Iron-gutted killjoy of a Dad;
Too well perhaps. Why did I let you groan

That rugged year, when you reached out to me
For help, down South? I thought, 'The lion's whelp
Must learn to fight the jackals without help'—
And you became a prefect. Sodomy

Is what they teach. I heard that little slut,
Your stepmother, after she'd piled me drunk
Under a blanket in my dogbox bunk,
Creep out to join you in the garden hut;

I never whispered of it. Muskets blazed
From the hunched snipers of pohutukawa
The day you stole my wallet and my car
And drove to Puhoi. Now I fumble dazed

Outside the door. O Absalom, the beast
Of anger, time and age will grind my skull
To powder! Spiders web your sailboat's hull.
The sword of Joab rages in the East.

THOUGHTS OF A
REMUERA HOUSEWIFE

The tranquillizers on my
glass-topped table, black-and-green
pomegranate seeds, belong to
Pluto, that rough king—so I
have eaten six, to go in
quietly, quietly through

the dark mirror to his world
of chaos and the grave—'Ann,
how strong you are!' my mother
said yesterday when the wild
pony all but threw Robin
under its hooves; I got her

to mount again. They don't know
I am Pluto's Queen. . . . Oh yes,
I kept your letter saying
it was no good—what did you
mean by that? The drugged clouds race
over the gun-pit facing

all storm, where you stopped the car
and undid my jersey—now
my husband is undressing
and jerking at his collar
with the Bugs Bunny grin I
hated so. . . . Our sort of dying

kept me young—my love, how high
the cocksfoot was! our own bed
walled in by soldier stalks of
grass—no one else could touch me,
among the lions' dens—mad,
happy, lost! In Pluto's cave

from granite thrones we watch the
ghosts whirling like snaking fog
quietly, quietly down
to their own urn, not to see
ever the sun's sweat-streaked flag
thunder again. . . . In London

do they play Schubert or Brahms
in asbestos rooms? Do girls
bite your throat? When you turned me
into a violin (dreams
are what I go by) that pulse
in your neck. . . . My Satan, why

did you not stay where flames rise
always up? You said no one
can fight the world. . . . No; it's not
a world at all, but Pluto's
iron-black star, the quiet
planet furthest from the sun.

HENLEY PUB
a traveller's soliloquy

Brown-bellied curtains, blood-beat of
The radiogram . . . I'll not forget
Your flat in Royal Terrace where the wet
Tom-kitten squealed at the porch door: you'd smile
And call him grizzle-guts . . . I drove
Drunk as a crocodile
At eighty round the bends to Henley
Under an asphalt moon. It's morning. Look:
The Taieri flood, Jehovah's book,
Ruffles its page, does not untwist our sin
Which is itself, the triple snarling grin
Of Cerberus. The barman's heel
Crushes a hot butt, and I
Burn. The vacillations of the sky
Shine through the brandy glass.
                                   Hail, holy Queen!
Beyond the serpent waves they glitter green,
Your willows on the far bank. Mother, my dream
Of God has died. The bog-black stream
Swallows time. Trout and eel
Are sliding through my rib-cage. They will eat
The self no fire could touch, your faithful deadbeat
Altar boy. One room
Contains the bandaged glory and the doom
Of Israel. In Father Hogan's box
I gripped the lion by the jowls,
Splitting her sin from mine to feed the fowls
Of judgement. Then wild bees among the rocks
Loaded miraculous honey in the white
Carcass.
         I loved you well,
Delilah; and I lost my hold on life
The day you burnt that letter from my wife.
Your body is my Hell.

59

The waves of the Taieri are bending bright;
A car and a man could go down
Easily under it. Last night in town,
The gin-glass empty on the floor,
I felt the rustle of the hunter's net—
A Swedish novel on the coverlet,
Your window open to the Leith Stream's roar,
Your head thrown back like one about to die,
Your body plump and bare—
I thought, shoving my muscle through black hair,
'What is a man, this glittering dung-fed fly
Who burrows in foul earth?'
                                        And that is all;
All; Jehovah's sky
And earth like millstones grind us small.

TOMCAT

This tomcat cuts across the
zones of the respectable
through fences, walls, following
other routes, his own. I see
the sad whiskered skull-mouth fall
wide, complainingly, asking

to be picked up and fed, when
I thump up the steps through bush
at 4 p.m. He has no
dignity, thank God! has grown
older, scruffier, the ash-
black coat sporting one or two

flowers like round stars, badges
of bouts and fights. The snake head
is seamed on top with rough scars:
old Samurai! He lodges
in cellars, and the tight furred
scrotum drives him into wars

as if mad, yet tumbling on
the rug looks female, Turkish-
trousered. His bagpipe shriek at
sluggish dawn dragged me out in
pyjamas to comb the bush
(he being under the vet

for septic bites): the old fool
stood, body hard as a board,
heart thudding, hair on end, at
the house corner, terrible,
yelling at something. They said,
'Get him doctored.' I think not.

A WISH FOR BERRIES

Today the waves of bright lead
lift rubbish, driftwood, in each
high bending wall: a good day
for gulls or dogs. The worn touch
of air and sun unkindly
like a dull whore tames the blood

offering only sleep. Yes . . .
I think of a friend who took
poison lately. Being dead,
he has gone into the dark
sheaf of truth and shares a word
with me just as my eyes close—

'Pity all things'—Do the tough
kids need pity who wrestle
under the bathing shed wall?
or the girls whose broad muscles
slide in bermuda shorts, all
intent on a thunder-proof

world of knowledge? I cannot
pity what is; but look up
at the karaka tree whose
thick wide leaves contain such ripe
yellow berries, their clusters
would take a fortnight to eat.

GREAT-UNCLES AND
GREAT-AUNTS

From Black Head to the bar of
Taieri Mouth, my father's
uncle scattered lupin seed
whose branches now give cover
to townbred couples who ride
out in cars, on bikes, and leave

pale condoms like balloons, or
shit among the fibred roots
that turn the dunes to soil—what
loose bright female bloom then fights
out of the bush's storm-wet
tabernacle! The colour

of blood or meditation
delicately hung, and the
pollen blown over the wide
stretch-marked belly of the sea—
Did strong chains in heart and head
choke back the airy dragon

that feeds on sighs, in those Job-
bearded crofters who split logs
for bluegum fences, and built
sod huts where now the gale brags?
Their bannock-meal lacking salt
grew mouldy—their wives could scrub

all stains from moleskin breeches
except Adam's dirt—and so
the lack ate inwardly like
fire in piled-up couchgrass too
green for it, billowing smoke—
a servant-girl's bruised haunches

up-ended in the barn, heads
split bloody at the caber-
tossing show—loud pipes, whisky . . .
O Mary, fetch a sugar
bag of snow to freshen my
great-aunts in their burning shrouds!

TO A PRINT OF
QUEEN VICTORIA

I advise rest; the farmhouse
we dug you up in has been
modernized, and the people
who hung you as their ikon
against the long passage wall
are underground—Incubus

and excellent woman, we
inherit the bone acre
of your cages and laws. This
dull green land suckled at your
blood's *frigor Anglicanus*,
crowning with a housewife's tally

the void of Empire, does not
remember you—and certain
bloody bandaged ghosts rising
from holes of Armageddon
at Gallipoli or Sling
Camp, would like to fire a shot

through the gilt frame. I advise
rest, Madam; and yet the tomb
holds much that we must travel
barely without. Your print—'from
an original pencil
drawing by the Marchioness

'of Granby, March, eighteen nine-
ty seven . . .' Little mouth, strong
nose and hooded eye—they speak
of half-truths my type have slung
out of the window, and lack
and feel the lack too late. Queen,

you stand most for the time of
early light, clay roads, great trees
unfelled, and the smoke from huts
where girls in sack dresses
stole butter . . . The small rain spits
today. You smile in your grave.

A FAMILY PHOTOGRAPH 1939

Waves bluster up the bay and through the throat
Of the one-span bridge. My brother shoots
The gap alone
Like Charon sculling in his boat
Above the squids and flounders. With the jawbone
Of a sperm whale he fights the town,
Dances on Fridays to the cello
With black-haired sluts. My father in his gumboots
Is up a ladder plucking down
The mottled autumn-yellow
Dangling torpedo clusters
Of passion fruit for home-made wine.
My mother in the kitchen sunshine
Tightens her dressing gown,
Chops up carrots, onions, leeks,
For thick hot winter soup. No broom or duster
Will shift the English papers piled on chairs
And left for weeks.
I, in my fuggy room at the top of the stairs,
A thirteen-year-old schizophrene,
Write poems, wish to die,
And watch the long neat mason-fly
Malignantly serene
Arrive with spiders dopier than my mind
And build his clay dungeons inside the roller blind.

SEVEN YEAR OLD POET
(after Rimbaud)

The mother, shutting the schoolbook, walked off blind
And well content, not seeing the hatred of work behind
The child's bumpy forehead, and under the blue eyes
An enemy self not built to fraternize.

Obedient he'd drudge all day; a quite
Intelligent boy; but somehow the sour bite
Of hypocrisy showed in his habits. Passing along
Mildewed passages, he'd stick out his tongue
And clench both fists in his groin, watching the spark
Of tiny specks that floated in the dark
Under his eyelids.
                    If a door on the evening air
Was open, you'd see him gasp, half up the stair,
Like a drying frog, under the gulf of day
That hung from the roofs. He'd hide himself away
In summer, clubbed flat, torpid, in the dell
Of a latrine, peacefully drinking the smell,
And it was cool there.
                    Sometimes when winter moonlight
Had washed the bushes, and antiseptic night
Drove out the daytime odours, he'd lie at the foot
Of a wall behind the house, like a cabbage root
Half underground, rubbing his eyes in order
To see visions, and hear each scabbed leaf shudder.
Quite tragic! His companions were those bent
Children whose clothes have a smell of excrement,
Old-fashioned, black-earth-knuckled, sometimes tooth-
    less,
Talking together in idiot gentleness.

And if, catching him out in some foul act
Of pity, his worrying Mother grubbed round the fact

For evidence, out of sick love he'd raise
A screen, and she'd believe it—that blue-eyed liar's
    gaze!

The seven-year-old would make up yarns inside
His own head, of the wastes where Freedom glows like
    a bride:
Savannahs, great trees, suns and shores—He'd rush
To coloured magazines, and stare and blush
At Spanish and Italian girls.
                              From time to time a wild
Tomboy, the next-door family's dragged-up child
Brown-eyed and skittish, would jump on his back from
    behind—
Just eight years old—tossing her plaits; and blind
As a weasel in a burrow, he'd use his teeth
To bite her bare arse from underneath
(She never wore pants)—then, bruised by her heels and
    her claws,
He'd mooch to his room with the taste of her flesh in
    his jaws.

Sundays in winter, hair flattened with brilliantine,
At the pedestal table, reading a salad-green-
Edged-Bible—he hated it. In the alcove at night
Millstone dreams would grind him, till day's light
Drying the sweats of terror, pink as a dove,
Came back to the gable.
                         God he did not love,
But men, men he saw at sunset, dark
From the sun's glare, strolling in smocks to the park
Where the town criers would make the crowd come
To grizzle or laugh at their words, by the thrice-heard
    roll of a drum.
—He dreamt of the grassy field, where light in waves
Rose up, with a smell like bread, from the groined caves

Waist-high, a place for love!
                                    And more than all else
He liked what is dark: as when, shut from the bells
In the barn of his room—not minding the icy damp
Of the blue walls, he would read of a rebel camp
Among drowned forests, leaden skies, great flowers
Of flesh in starry woods, Andean towers,
Giddiness, flight—while the street chattered below—
Face down, his blue eyes flickering to and fro,
He would live the novel—alone, stretched out on the
    pale
Coarse linen that caught the wind, a ship in full sail!

THE FIRST COMMUNIONS
after Rimbaud

1

It makes me want to laugh, those country churches
Where fifteen kids like ugly ducklings
Dirty the pillars, quack, talk back
To an old daft priest in greasy shoes:
Being instructed!
                 And the sun glitters through leaves;
Light roosts in the windows like broken loaves.

The stone smells always of the earth it came from;
Boulders just like these are piled
Where the earth trembles on heat.
                      Rose-bushes, briars
Climb over them, and the heavy-headed wheat
Pushes up through the crevices
In the belly of the ground, the earth's old dried scars.

Once in a hundred years they wash these churches,
Like barns, with curds of milk and blue water.
Flies out of the pub and the cowshed gather
To eat the wax of candle-droppings
Down there, below the peeled paint
Of Madonna and Saint.

But the kids must think of their Dads and Mums
Each doing a lifetime of hard labour:
Good peasant stock!
              They scat, with red necks crawling where
Christ's Priest has touched them: Old Iron Fingers. He
   goes glum
To a house shaded by sycamores
And well paid for. The kids are alive in the sun

71

For a day at least.
                    O first black suits! Jam tarts!
Plates on doilies under Napoleon's picture
For the Josephs and the Marthas who'll meet at the
     rail
With tongues stuck out, two halves of a map
That's not yet one.
                    The First Communion's flow of sap
Will come and go, and these things remain.

The girls who sit prim on the church benches are glad
When the boys whisper, 'Little bitches!'
Like monkeys in new jackets after Mass
Or sung Vespers, the brats crowd out
Snapping their fingers and jumping, singing bad
     ditties
At those shop-window dummies, the families in cafés.

In the meantime the fat old Priest picks out
A holy picture for each child.
He walks in his garden when the air is mild
And hears the fiddle-twang downstreet
Of distant dancing. He sketches a step; in his old bull's
     breast the night
Plunders like a bandit the gold towers of light.

2

One pupil he has noticed among the catechised
(Mostly children of the nobs)—
A strange little girl with sad eyes
And a white forehead. Her Dad has a caretaker's job.
'On that dear head, a Rachel among the catechised,
God will pour down His grace like a waterfall.'

3

The child's not well. She fidgets. Not yet inside the
  grim
Church, that cave of echoes, she is visited by
A shuddering fit. On the bed in her small high
Attic she dreams of the conquering Victim.

'I am dying', she whispers; crosses her hands and waits,
The smart one, stealing a march on the other girls.
Angels, Jesuses, Virgins whiter than pearl
Float through the ceiling. Her soul has opened its gates.

Adonai! .... He rides on the rolling crest
Of Latin words. Green lightnings jump from the ice-
  browed
Sky. The stars are wrapped in a scrubbed white shroud
Mottled with blood from a virgin martyr's breast.

A child's vow of virginity made in a dream!
She bites on the freezing wafer of Ransom,
Purer than moats of lilies, fresher than ice-cream,
O Queen of Angels, your ice-crystals of pardon!

4

But the Virgin goes back into the book;
Often enough a prayer can snap like a stalk. ...
All she has left is an old missal's vellum,
A vile wood-cut, and the bronze-clad giant of Boredom.

And a vague wish like a wind begins to flurry
The chaste blue dream (rough as the hair of a goat
Saint Joseph's beard)—it tugs at the seamless coat
With which Christ hides a nude and human body.

She is yearning, yearning towards the core of the fur-
nace,
Gripping the pillow tight to smother her cries,
Struggling in the net of a self-made paradise,
Mouth wet. . . . The yards are loaded with faggots of
darkness.

The kid reaches the end of her tether. With one
Hand, arching her body, she opens the blue
Bed-curtain, to let the fresh air through
On belly and breast that bake in the holy oven . . .

5
Later—waking at midnight—the window is gleaming
White; in the curtain's fold the moon drowns deep;
The whiteness of Sunday beckons her soul from sleep
To walk. She has had red dreams; and her nose is
bleeding.

Hollow and pure, she raises the vase of her heart
To God, and thirsts for the taste of the dark fountain
That flows all night from a cleft in Moses' mountain
And heals the wounded earth. She hides in the skirt

Of the first Mother, unseeable Night, who gathers
All young hurt things into her cloudy arms;
She thirsts for the Night, whose waters of grey calm
Cannot be stained by the blood of human fever.

Victim and little wife—her star watches her walk
With a candle in her hand down to the courtyard
Where a jacket is hanging on a line above the hard
Stones. . . . Her small ghost hears the ghosts of the
roofs talk.

6

Her God's-night was spent in a shithouse under the sky.
Through holes in the roof the white air crowded in
To the fluttering candle, and a wild vine
Tumbled over a broken wall nearby;

And later yet, when low skies plated the bones
Of the houses with gold, and the steam of washing
  water
Dusted the shadows with a stink like sulphur,
A living heart of light glowed on the stones . . .

7

Who will speak the epitaph of pity,
Eaters of dung, warpers of all things made,
You hypocrites?—Will you spit at the walking dead
When her leper's clapper sounds in the tomb of the city?

8

When she has swallowed down the green sour fruit,
One sword-grey dawn, sad in the yoke of love,
She will see her man still hunched up, dreaming of
A million sky-born Marys, and cry out:

'Do you know I have killed you? I have taken
Mouth, heart, whatever a man is,
And I am rotting. Oh, to lie down loveless
In the waters of night, with the Dead, and never waken!

'I was young once, and Christ made me foul.
He crammed my throat with what I spew up now.
You've kissed my Gideon's Fleece; you've nuzzled my
  brow;
And I let it happen. . . . A good time had by all!

'Men! You men! You don't know how it is:
How every woman is torn in half between
The conscience and the flesh. We roast in pain,
God's whores, each one of us, burnt black by kisses.

'At my first Communion I married the Cross.
Your touch, your words of love, are a shut book.
Think. My soul, and the flesh that you took,
Are boiling with maggot-white kisses of Jesus!'

9
And the soul that rots and the soul that lacks light
Will feel Your hatred grip them like a nurse,
Having lain down on the bed of Your granite Curse,
From mountains of Eden rolling towards the night.

O Christ, Christ, You have taken our strength from us!
You pale God, nailing to Your altar bone
Since Golgotha the women You turn to stone,
Chained to the earth in grief, mounted by the incubus!

THE CHERRY TREE
for John Weir

Uphill, uphill, beyond the
sluice-boxes, pipes and sacking
roots of old man broom had kneed
apart—so high above the
gully, one hose-nozzle could
have sent the whole cliff tumbling,

just at noon, when sheep skulls were
alive with cicadas, I
came to that uncertain tree
of wild black cherries. Under
the rock crest, bare to the sky,
grass-overgrown, and like the

clods of ruined Carthage thrown
into time's trench, lay sod walls
built by an Irishman—what
had been a croft. The sluice-blown
chasm gashed the small path that
led once by hives and kennels

to a hill orchard. Only
that dry tree was left. Half a
mile in air, above the cliff,
the dams, the broken ground, the
wide island, as if brought safe
on a hawk's back, high up there

I tasted bitter cherries
at noon, poised alone among
crooked branches. Did I then
catch in the drunken abyss
wind-shaken, the cry of one
bird or spirit with no nesting

place between dark sky and burst
acres of rummaged clay? If
so, I should have made the sign
of the cross on forehead, breast
and shoulders, to split off, John,
the dead grief from the live grief.

GUY FAWKES NIGHT

I saw the freckled children burn their guy
In dry November by the reddened waves
That wash the doorsteps of the dead. Our graves
Are tinder. Look, the sacking falls apart,
The straw will catch as the leopard flames jump high
And grip the squib-plugged heart
Of the poor guy. The dead who have no names
Are shouting, *Miserere!* from the flames,
The sheep of Calvin, clipped for Judgement Day;
Poseidon hammers on their house of clay,

Laird, bullock-driver, wife in stiff black gown
And kitchen hussy. In the scrubwood pyre
They suffer, Lady. Hoist them from the fire
And give them water—water for that old
Worm-eaten Adam with an iron crown,
An Odin of the sheepfold
My great-granduncle set upon a gatepost
To guard his dying mana. Through the Host
They climb to God. Your Child laughs on my tongue
Among the trampled hay and cattle dung.

NEW ZEALAND
for Monte Holcroft

These unshaped islands, on the sawyer's bench,
Wait for the chisel of the mind,
Green canyons to the south, immense and passive,
Penetrated rarely, seeded only
By the deer-culler's shot, or else in the north
Tribes of the shark and the octopus,
Mangroves, black hair on a boxer's hand.

The founding fathers with their guns and bibles,
Botanist, whaler, added bones and names
To the land, to us a bridle
As if the id were a horse: the swampy towns
Like dreamers that struggle to wake,

Longing for the poet's truth
And the lover's pride. Something new and old
Explores its own pain, hearing
The rain's choir on curtains of grey moss
Or fingers of the Tasman pressing
On breasts of hardening sand, as actors
Find their own solitude in mirrors,

As one who has buried his dead,
Able at last to give with an open hand.

ON READING YEVTUSHENKO

When the mine exploded at Kaitangata
Trucks flew out as if from the barrel of a gun,
Trucks and truckers, bodies of men,
Or so my father told me;
                and far down
In those dark passages they heard faintly
The waves of the sea hammer
Above their heads.
            My father's hands are corded
With swollen veins, but my hands are thinner
And my thoughts are cold, Zhenya Yevtushenko;
They are covered with black dust.
                Reading you
I remember our own strangled Revolution:
1935. The body of our Adam was dismembered
By statisticians.
             I would like to meet you
Quietly in a café, where hoboes and freckled girls
Drink, talk; not to pump you; only to revalue in your
   company
Explosions, waves of the sea.

FISHERMEN

I invent nothing.
               Those men in oilskins
Won't ever stagger up the beach
And drop their bundles. Those who believed
Only in the sea and themselves—
Norwegian Maoris—one was dragged down
When his gumboots filled;
                        another's boat
Struck the sandbar at low tide,
Drunk, with a load of fish and manuka.
                           Mention
In their obituaries the economic factor:
An octopus whose blood is money
The National Mortgage owned their boats and bodies,
But there is something else.
                  A noise like thunder
Beyond the dune, an overflowing
Shout:
      US!
                 And the hands of the sea
Lifting the long black hair of a man floating.

THE WAVES

I

Accepted here, here only,
For what one is, not the chalk mask,
Gentility of a robot or a clown,
But the sad mandrake torn
From earth, getting no likely truce on earth,
The brat of sighs, less wise than the afterbirth,
The one who should have not perhaps been born.

The wave ignores, consoles, flowing and ebbing
Without reflection. Sand or oven ash
Trickling from the roots of matted swordgrass
Count thirty-seven years between
The sweet first spout of milk and this dried-up
Poem with no breasts, my concubine.

The wave bangs in channels of gnarled stone.

2

The island like an old cleft skull
With tussock and bone needles on its forehead
Lives in the world before the settlers came
With gun and almanac.
                              One half-mad
Solitary six-foot fisherman
Blasted a passage out with gelignite
Between the shore and the island templebone
To let his boat come in, changing the drift
Of water from the bay.
                              There are veins of gold
In the reef below the sand.
                              I heard
Often, when young, the dialogue

83

Of wave with wave contending in that gullet
Where now the mussel-pickers go
Safely because the tide is low:
The strangled weight of sex and intellect
Contending and rejected in the cave
Where under weed gates the white octopus
Haunter and waker of the coast
In storms of genesis contains his power.

3
The sound of the sea would enter
That book-lined upper room,
Penetrating the convict dream
Of wordy love, as ropes of semen
Hang useless in the man's groin,
Or the bluebottle husk on the pane
Judged by the spider.

The slow language of the waves
Gave hope of truth to come,
Wideness, a dark meeting
With a woman with a body like the moon,
The mouths of water speaking
Putting aside the barren peace
Of those who are naked only in their graves.

4
At high tide I the burning
Mandrake coffinless stood
And saw the moon stride over
The belly of the flood
Against the tide's turning,
The horned and processional
Goddess of sexual pain
Who kills the mandrake I.

Though every stone and shell
Blazed in the superhuman
Arrows of light that fell
From the double axe and skull,
Lest I should be turned to rock
Or as a serpent glide
Or howl in a wolf's hide,
I called aloud for one
Living and breathing woman
To stand between and cover
My body with her own,
But there was none alive
Between the sea and the rock,
And my own lass who lay
At peace in her deft room,
Being curbed by gentility
Would never rise and run
Down over the black dune
With her grass-green skirt at her knee
To grip the burning ghost,
To lie with the naked man.
That huntress in the sky
Strode on, strode on,
The tide swung back, and I
Under the shade of a green bank stood
With poison crystals whirling in my blood
From the arrow in the breastbone.

5

How to distinguish from the flux of fire,
Salt tides and air, some ruler
Other than octopus, man-killing moon
Or our own twist of thought, breeds pain.
Wings of the albatross whose shadow
Lies on the seas at noon

I take as the type of a spirit bent
By abstract solitude,
Accepting all. The waves do not debase
Or drown what shares their fluid motion,
Yet hard for human blood

Is the habit of relinquishment,
Abandoning of Isaac to the knife
That tortured Abraham. Come now;
Poems are trash, the flesh I love will die,
Desire is bafflement,
But one may say that father Noah kept
Watch while the wild beasts slept,

Not knowing even if land would rise
Out of the barren waves.
That ark I keep, that watch on the edge of sleep,
While the dark water heaves.